Bald Eagles
A Chemical Nightmare

by Meish Goldish

Consultant: Bob Hatcher
Eagle Consultant to the American Eagle Foundation (www.eagles.org)
and Retired Nongame and Endangered Wildlife Coordinator (1978–2001)
Tennessee Wildlife Resources Agency

BEARPORT PUBLISHING

New York, New York

Credits

Cover and Title Page, © Mervyn Rees/Alamy; 4, © Stephen Mcsweeny/Shutterstock; 5, © Bettmann/Corbis; 6, © John Eastcott & Yva Momatiuk/National Geographic/ Getty Images; 7A, © R. Gino Santa Maria/Shutterstock; 7B, © Tadija/Shutterstock; 7C, © James E. Knopf/Shutterstock; 8, © Paul Nicklen/National Geographic/Getty Images; 9, © Jim Brandenburg/Minden Pictures; 10, © AP Images; 11, © Richard Day/ Animals Animals-Earth Scenes; 12, © 2007 Lon Lauber/AlaskaStock.com; 13, © Leo Keeler/Accent Alaska; 14, © Ken Cole/Animals Animals-Earth Scenes; 15, © Robert Falls Photography; 16, © Erich Schlegel/Dallas Morning News/Corbis; 17, © Werner Forman/Art Resource, NY; 18, © Marsha Wilson/ Animals Animals-Earth Scenes; 20, © Cary Anderson/Accent Alaska; 21, © Fish & Wildlife Service; 22, © William Munoz; 23, © William Munoz; 24, © Bill Clark/Roll Call Photos/Newscom.com; 25, © John Edwards/Getty Images; 26, © Dorothy Keeler/Accent Alaska; 27, Courtesy of NASA Kennedy Space Center; 28, © Tony Campbell/Shutterstock; 29A, © Michael Dick/ Animals Animals-Earth Scenes; 29B, © David Hodges/Alamy; 31, © Arlene Jean Gee/ Shutterstock.

Publisher: Kenn Goin
Senior Editor: Lisa Wiseman
Creative Director: Spencer Brinker
Photo Researcher: Amy Dunleavy
Cover Design: Dawn Beard Creative

Library of Congress Cataloging-in-Publication Data

Goldish, Meish.
  Bald eagles : a chemical nightmare / by Meish Goldish.
    p. cm. — (America's animal comebacks)
  Includes bibliographical references and index.
  ISBN-13: 978-1-59716-505-1 (library binding)
  ISBN-10: 1-59716-505-0 (library binding)
  1. Bald eagle—Effects of pesticides on—Juvenile literature. I. Title.

  QL696.F32G65 2008
  598.9'42—dc22

                            2007009751

For more information, write to Bearport Publishing Company, Inc., 101 Fifth Avenue, Suite 6R, New York, New York 10003. Printed in the United States of America in North Mankato, Minnesota.

042011
040111CGC

10 9 8 7 6 5 4

Contents

Stopping a Killer

More than 50 years ago, a mystery puzzled American **wildlife** officials. The bald eagle **population** was dropping sharply throughout the United States. No one could figure out why.

A bald eagle is not bald. In Old English, *balde* means white.

Then a bird lover named Charles Broley made a discovery. While studying bald eagles in Florida in the 1940s and 1950s, he noticed that there were fewer young birds each year. Broley believed that the problem was due to a chemical called DDT. Could anything be done to save the eagles?

Charles Broley

Bald eagles live only in North America. They are found in every state in the United States except Hawaii.

A Better Past

Life was not always so bad for bald eagles. In the 1600s, between 250,000 and 500,000 bald eagles flew freely in North America. **Native Americans** praised the bird for its beauty. They admired its speed and strength. They respected its **keen** eyesight and hunting skills.

A bald eagle uses its speed and sharp claws to catch food.

A bald eagle in the sky can see a rabbit on the ground from two miles (3.2 km) away. From high in the air, it can spot a fish under water.

After the United States became a nation in 1776, Americans continued to honor the bald eagle. In 1782, it was named the national bird. The eagle appeared on U.S. coins and bills. It became a symbol of freedom for America. So how did things turn so bad for this special bird?

The bald eagle appears on U.S. paper money and even on passports.

The Trouble Begins

Bald eagles started facing serious trouble in the 1700s. Many people began moving across America. They settled on land where bald eagles lived. People cut down trees to build houses, towns, and farms. Since the birds built their nests in the trees, they now had to find other places to live.

Bald eagles build nests high in trees to watch for food and enemies.

The eagles faced other dangers as well. Many farmers and ranchers believed that bald eagles were attacking their **livestock** or eating too many fish. Some paid hunters to go after the birds. For the next 200 years, many bald eagles were killed.

Bald eagles hunt small animals such as fish, rabbits, and birds. They do not attack big animals like sheep or cows. However, they will sometimes eat large animals that they did not kill.

A New Problem

In the 1940s, bald eagles faced a new problem. Americans began to use a **pesticide** called DDT. Farmers sprayed it on crops and livestock to kill insects. Home owners sprayed it on their grass to get rid of bugs.

DDT was very powerful. One spray killed hundreds of pests. Yet its power did not end there.

DDT kills insects that might destroy a farmer's crop or harm livestock.

Rain washed DDT into rivers and streams. The pesticide built up in fish and other animals that ate smaller creatures from the waters.

Bald eagles ate the poisoned animals. DDT entered their bodies. The chemical was very harmful to the birds.

DDT stays dangerous as it travels from animal to animal.

The bald eagle is a **bird of prey**. It uses its sharp beak and claws to hunt for food.

Danger for Babies

DDT robbed the bald eagles' bodies of **calcium**. A female bird needs calcium to lay eggs with strong shells. Females with DDT laid eggs with thin, weak shells. Often, parents crushed their eggs while sitting on them. Many **eaglets** died in their shells before hatching. Sometimes an egg would break inside the female's body before it was even laid.

An eaglet uses a hard bump on its beak to crack open its shell from the inside.

A bald eagle egg **hatches** in about 35 days. The parents take turns sitting on the egg during that time.

The number of young bald eagles soon began to **decline**. Then, as eagles started to die of old age, the total number of these birds dropped sharply. By 1963, there were only 417 pairs of bald eagles in the **lower United States**. Something had to be done to save them.

A bald eagle feeds its eaglets several times a day.

A Big Discovery

At the time, people did not know that DDT was hurting bald eagles. Wildlife officials tried to protect the birds in other ways. New laws were passed. It became **illegal** to hunt, kill, or own a bald eagle, its eggs, or feathers. The laws helped save some bald eagles. Yet many still continued to die.

After 1940, people were not allowed to harm bald eagles.

During the 1940s and 1950s, Charles Broley studied bald eagles to find out what was harming them. He counted the birds each year. In 1946, he was able to find 150 young eagles. However, something changed the following year. The number of birds that he found dropped to about 80. This number continued to get lower each year. Broley strongly believed that the decrease in birds was related to DDT. The chemical caused there to be fewer and fewer eagles in the wild.

In 1939, Broley started putting leg bands on eagles. The bands helped him study and keep track of the eagles.

Scientists agreed with Broley's discovery. In 1967, the bald eagle was declared an **endangered species**. In 1972, the United States **banned** DDT.

Special Feathers

Native Americans welcomed the ban on DDT. However, the law against owning eagle feathers caused a problem. Many Native American groups use the feathers in their religious **ceremonies**.

Luckily, a solution was found. In the 1970s, U. S. officials opened the National Eagle Repository in Denver, Colorado. Native American groups could now go there to get the feathers they needed.

A Native American performs the Eagle Dance.

No eagles are hunted or killed for these special feathers. They come from eagles that lost feathers or died in other ways. This allows bald eagles living in the wild to remain safe.

The feathers that Native Americans use cannot be sold or traded. Instead, they are passed down over the years to younger tribe members.

An eagle feather war bonnet

A bald eagle has about 7,000 feathers on its body.

A Steady Growth

The 1972 ban on DDT was very helpful to bald eagles. Their numbers soon began to increase. By 1974, there were almost 800 pairs of bald eagles **mating** in the lower United States. Their population had nearly doubled in just ten years! Over time, the number of bald eagles increased even more.

A bald eagle family

Bald eagles mate for life. If one dies, the other eagle finds a new partner.

In 1995, officials changed the listing for bald eagles. It went from *endangered* to *threatened*. Eagles are no longer in immediate danger of becoming **extinct**. However, *threatened* means they could become endangered again soon. Scientists now watch the birds closely to see how their numbers change.

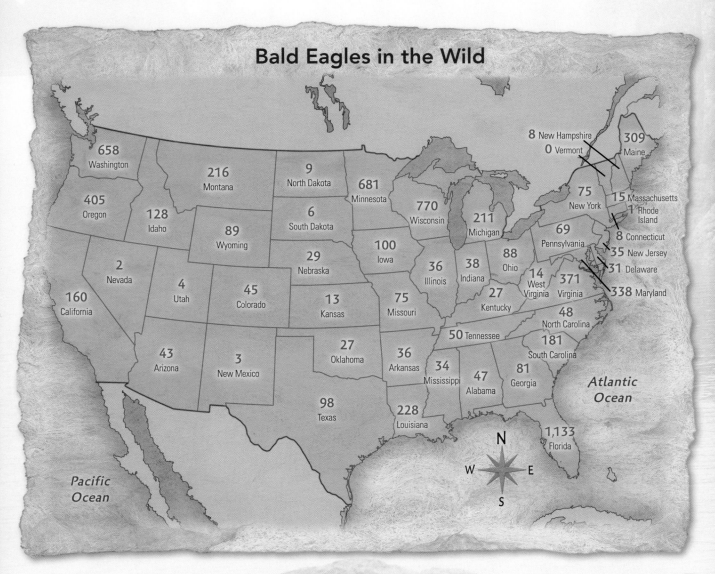

Bald Eagles in the Wild

658 Washington
216 Montana
9 North Dakota
681 Minnesota
8 New Hampshire
0 Vermont
309 Maine
405 Oregon
128 Idaho
6 South Dakota
770 Wisconsin
75 New York
15 Massachusetts
1 Rhode Island
89 Wyoming
211 Michigan
69 Pennsylvania
8 Connecticut
35 New Jersey
2 Nevada
29 Nebraska
100 Iowa
88 Ohio
31 Delaware
160 California
4 Utah
45 Colorado
13 Kansas
75 Missouri
36 Illinois
38 Indiana
14 West Virginia
371 Virginia
338 Maryland
27 Kentucky
48 North Carolina
43 Arizona
3 New Mexico
27 Oklahoma
36 Arkansas
50 Tennessee
181 South Carolina
98 Texas
34 Mississippi
47 Alabama
81 Georgia
228 Louisiana
1,133 Florida

Atlantic Ocean

N
W E
S

Pacific Ocean

This map shows the number of bald eagle pairs found in the lower United States today.

Safe Homes

In order to keep increasing their numbers, bald eagles need safe homes. Most eagles live in Alaska. In 1982, state officials there created the Chilkat Bald Eagle **Preserve**. Here, 48,000 acres (19,425 hectares) of land are set aside for these birds. The preserve has many streams with salmon for the birds to eat.

More than 35,000 bald eagles live in Alaska. Many are in the Chilkat Bald Eagle Preserve.

Another safe home for bald eagles was set up in Maryland in 1976. The Patuxent Wildlife Research Center began to **breed** baby eagles. The program was a big success. It produced 124 new bald eagles. They were raised in **captivity** and then set free in different parts of the United States. The new birds went on to breed even more bald eagles.

Many bald eagles were hatched at the Patuxent Wildlife Research Center in Maryland.

A female bald eagle lays one to three eggs a year.

Helpful Scientists

Scientists such as Brian Mealey and Greta Parks continue to keep a close eye on bald eagles. They take blood samples of the young before they leave the nest. They also place a tag on each bird so they can identify it later on.

Brian Mealey and Greta Parks tag a young bald eagle so they can find and study it again later.

Mealey and Parks study the blood in their lab in Florida. They look at the chemicals found in it. They can tell if a bird is getting enough healthy food and water. The blood helps them learn more about the eagle's **habitat** and how to treat the bird if it gets sick.

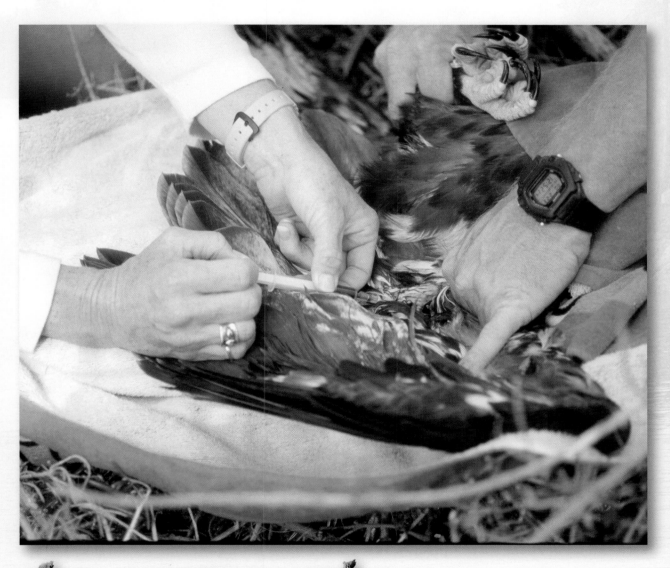

Florida has the most bald eagles of any state in the lower United States.

Brian Mealey holds down an eagle while Greta Parks takes a sample of blood.

An American Hero

Bald eagles continue to be a big part of American history. One very special bird is Challenger. As an eaglet, he was rescued during a storm in Louisiana in 1989. Unable to survive on his own, he was raised by people at the American Eagle Foundation. This group works to keep all eagles safe.

Challenger flies near the Capitol building in Washington, D.C.

Today, Challenger travels around the United States. He helps raise people's awareness of bald eagles and their need to be protected.

Challenger has another job, too. He was the first eagle trained to fly into sports stadiums during the singing of the National Anthem. He has even flown proudly at the Olympics. Challenger is an American hero!

Challenger has met many important people, including President Bill Clinton.

Challenger has been a guest at the White House in Washington, D.C.

The Future

Bald eagles have made much progress in recent years. Today, more than 8,000 pairs of mating bald eagles are found in the lower United States. About 70,000 birds live in Alaska and Canada.

The birds, however, still face great dangers. DDT is banned, yet other harmful chemicals are now found in many rivers and streams. Wildlife officials are working to fix this problem.

Another threat to bald eagles is electric power lines. Many birds die when they rest on them. Some companies are now burying their lines underground or building safe platforms for the birds.

Today, states are setting aside more land for bald eagles. With everyone's help, the bald eagle will remain a proud symbol of America.

A bald eagle can die if its wings accidentally touch electric power lines.

Eagles make the biggest nests of any bird in North America. These nests can sometimes be the size of a small car.

Bald Eagle Facts

In 1973, Congress passed the Endangered Species Act. This law protects animals and plants that are in danger of dying out in the United States. Harmful activities, such as hunting, capturing, or collecting endangered species, are illegal under this act.

The bald eagle was one of the first animals listed under the Endangered Species Act. Here are some other facts about this bird.

Population: North American population in the 1600s: **250,000–500,000**
North American population today: **70,000–100,000**

Weight	Wingspan	Length	Colors	
6–14 pounds (2.7–6.3 kg)	6–8 feet (1.8–2.4 m)	30–36 inches (76–91 cm) from tip of beak to tip of tail	Adult eagles: white head and tail; dark brown body	Young eagles: brown head, body, and tail; dark beak

Food	Life Span	Habitat
Mainly fish; also rabbits, squirrels, birds, snakes, and ducks	Up to 39 years in the wild; over 50 years in captivity	North America, mostly in Canada and Alaska

Other Eagles in Danger

Bald eagles are one kind of eagle making a comeback by increasing its numbers. Other types of eagles are also trying to make a comeback.

Harpy Eagle

- The harpy eagle is the largest kind of eagle. Its claws are as big as a bear's claws.

- Harpy eagles are very rare. Their current population is not known. About 50 nests have been found in Guyana, Venezuela, and Panama, all countries in South America.

- Harpy eagles are the national bird of Panama.

- Breeding programs and public education are helping these eagles make a comeback.

Philippine Eagle

- The Philippine eagle is the second largest of all eagles. There are fewer than 500 left in the wild.

- Philippine eagles live in the Philippines. The Philippine eagle is the national bird of the country.

- Breeding management and educational programs are helping these eagles make a comeback.

Glossary

banned (BAND) not allowed to be used

bird of prey (BURD UHV PRAY) a bird that hunts other animals for food

breed (BREED) to produce young

calcium (KAL-see-uhm) a chemical element found in bones and teeth

captivity (kap-TIV-uh-*tee*) a place where animals are kept so they cannot travel freely

ceremonies (SER-uh-*moh*-neez) events that mark a special occasion

decline (di-KLINE) to become fewer in number

eaglets (EE-glits) eagles that are too young to fly

endangered species (en-DAYN-jurd SPEE-sheez) a type of animal that is in danger of dying out completely

extinct (ek-STINGKT) when a kind of plant or animal has died out; no more of its kind is living anywhere in the world

habitat (HAB-uh-*tat*) a place in nature where an animal lives

hatches (HACH-iz) when an eggshell cracks open so that a baby can come out

illegal (i-LEE-guhl) against the law

keen (KEEN) able to notice things very well

livestock (LIVE-*stok*) animals raised on a farm or ranch, such as horses, sheep, and cows

lower United States (LOH-ur yoo-NITE-id STATES) all U.S. states except Alaska and Hawaii

mating (MAYT-ing) coming together to produce babies

Native Americans (NAY-tiv uh-MER-uh-kinz) the first people to live in America; they are sometimes called American Indians

pesticide (PESS-tuh-side) a chemical used to kill insects and bugs

population (*pop*-yuh-LAY-shuhn) the number of people or animals living in a place

preserve (pri-ZURV) a place where animals are kept safe and protected

wildlife (WILDE-life) wild animals living in their natural setting

Bibliography

DeFries, Cheryl L. *The Bald Eagle.* Berkeley Heights, NJ: Enslow (2003).

Dudley, Karen. *Bald Eagles.* Austin, TX: Raintree Steck-Vaughn (1998).

Evert, Laura. *Eagles.* Minnetonka, MN: NorthWord Press (2001).

Read More

Hodge, Deborah. *Eagles.* Tonowanda, NY: Kids Can Press (2000).

Morrison, Gordon. *Bald Eagle.* Boston: Houghton Mifflin (1998).

Patent, Dorothy Hinshaw. *The Bald Eagle Returns.* New York: Clarion Books (2000).

Priebe, Mac. *The Bald Eagle: Endangered No More.* Norwalk, CT: Mindfull Publishing (2000).

Learn More Online

To learn more about bald eagles, visit
www.bearportpublishing.com/AnimalComebacks

Index

About the Author

Meish Goldish has written more than 100 books for children.
He lives in Brooklyn, New York, where the *Brooklyn Daily Eagle*
is a popular newspaper.